Introduction

Hello smart kids,
before starting the connect the dots puzzles, we would like to explain the rules of this activity book. Are you ready? Let's go!

● ● ● ● ● ● ● ● ● ● ● ● ● ● ●

To make sure that you're getting the best results, you will need:

| To connect the dots. | To keep the line the same. | To fix mistakes. | To make straight lines. |

● ● ● ● ● ● ● ● ● ● ● ● ● ●

How to connect the dots in this book?

- Starting at number "1" connect the dots in sequential order.
- When you come across "X" stop connecting.
- After reaching "X" continue again from the following number (See example on the next page).
- These puzzles are challenging, when you feel tired - take a break and come back when you're ready.
- After connecting all the dots - colour the image!

Example

This example demonstrates how to properly connect the dots in this book. After reading this, you're ready to start connecting the dots!

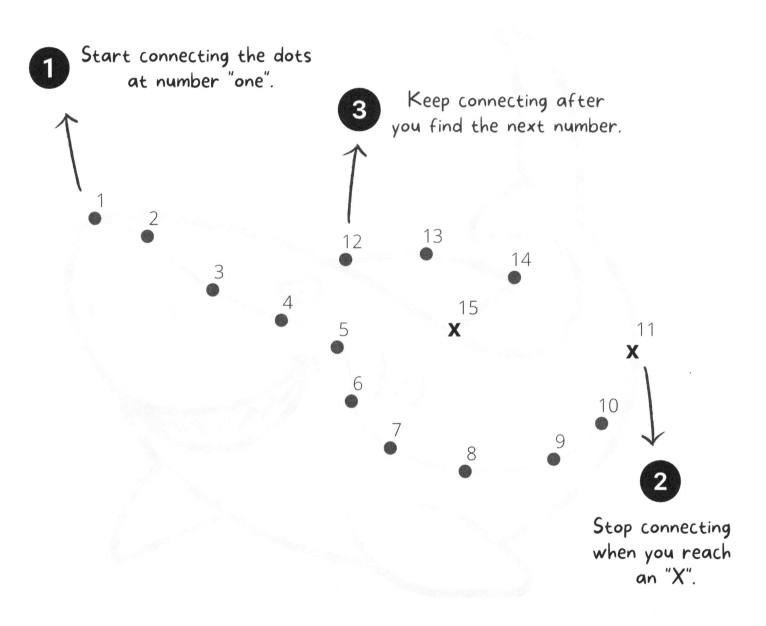

1 Start connecting the dots at number "one".

3 Keep connecting after you find the next number.

2 Stop connecting when you reach an "X".

Enjoy!

Figure 1

Figure 2

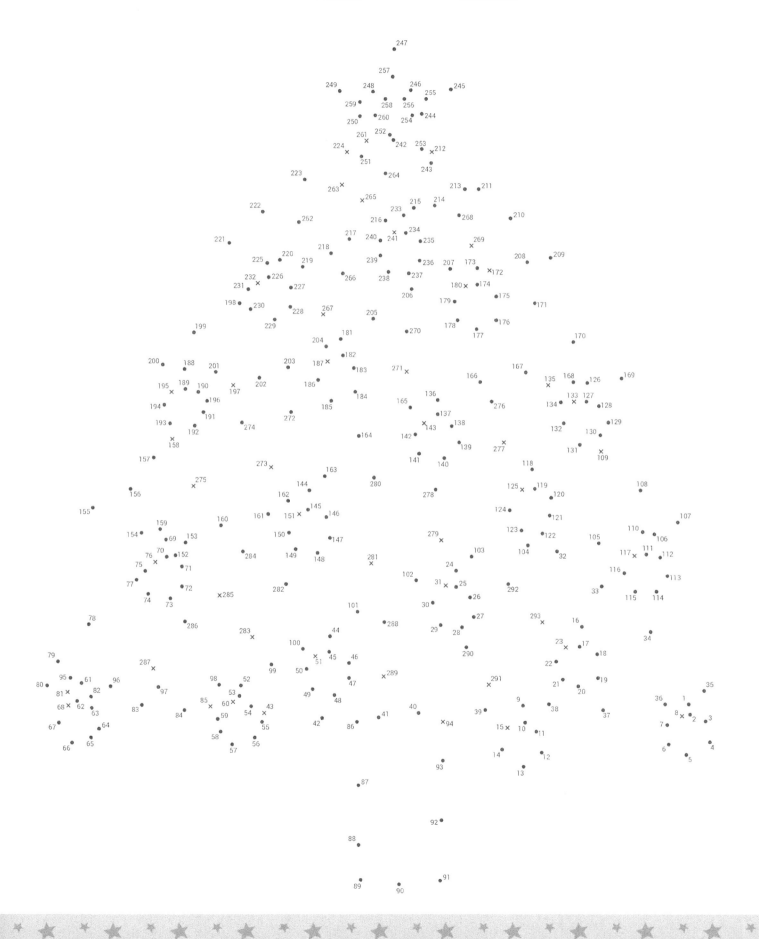

Figure 3

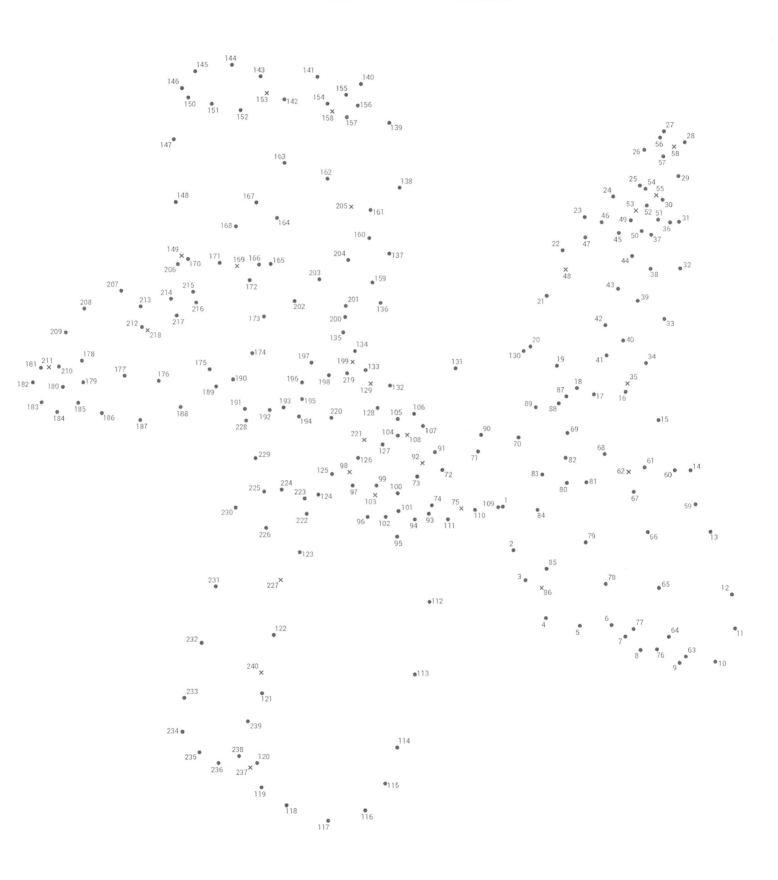

Figure 4

Figure 5

Super Challenging!

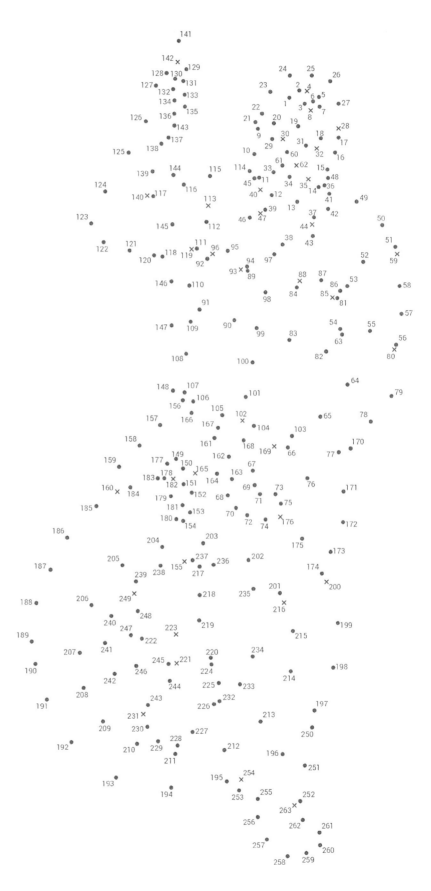

Figure 6

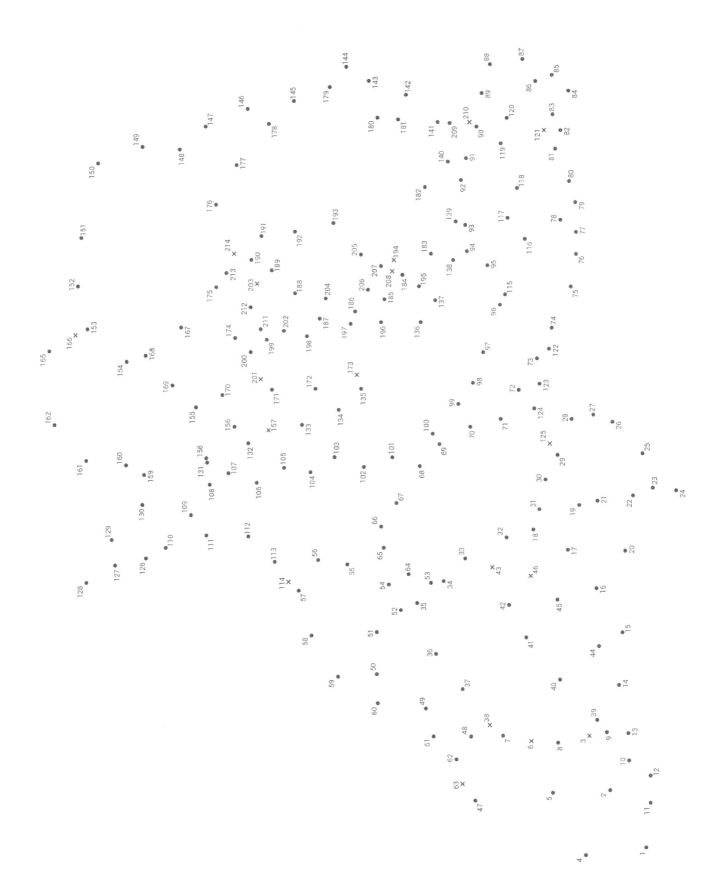

Figure 7

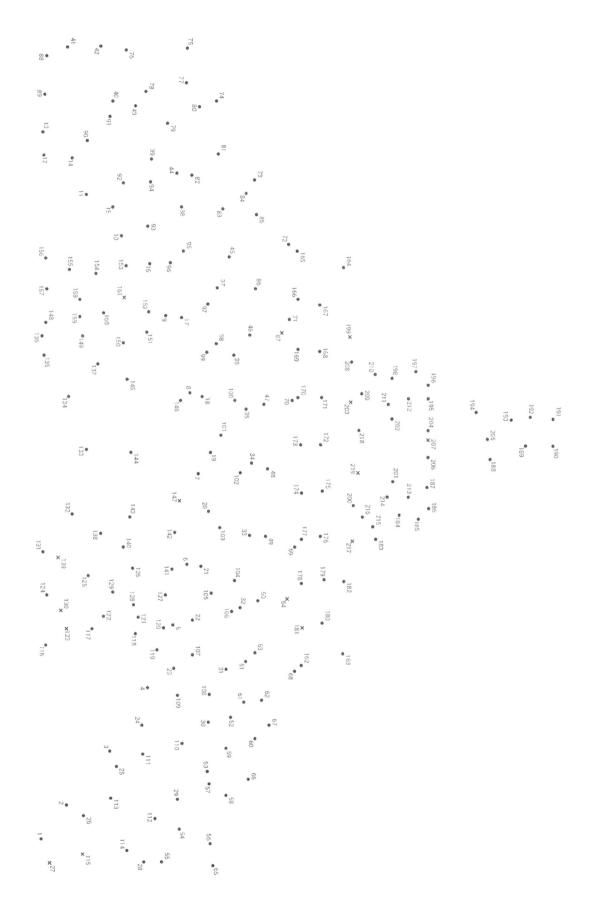

Figure 8

Figure 9

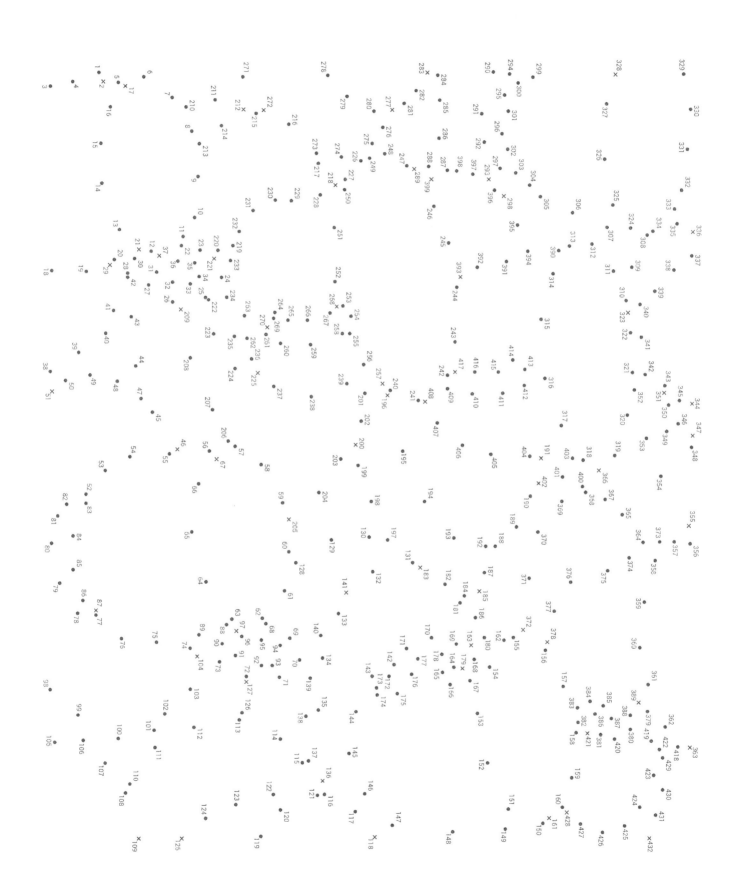

Figure 10

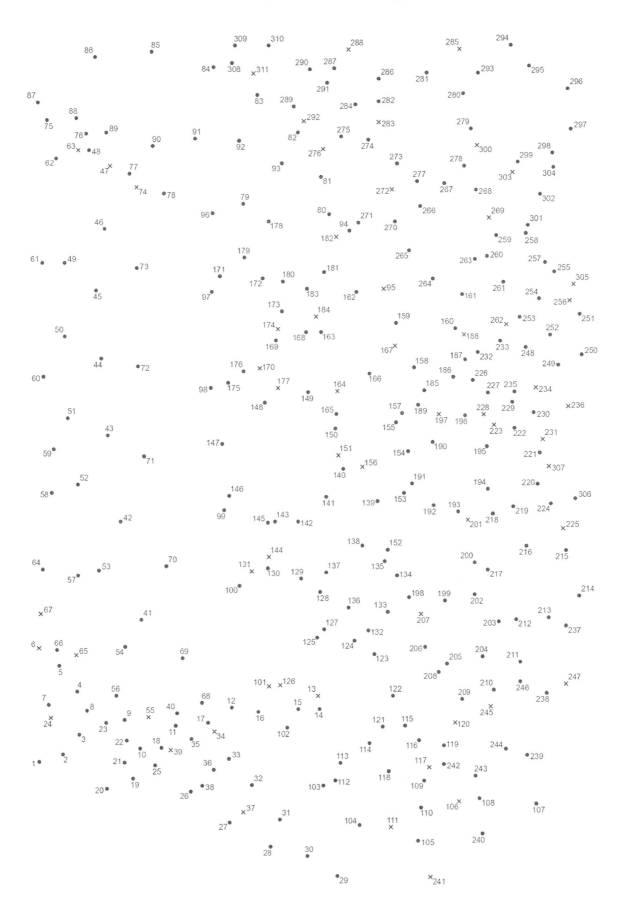

Figure 11

Figure 12

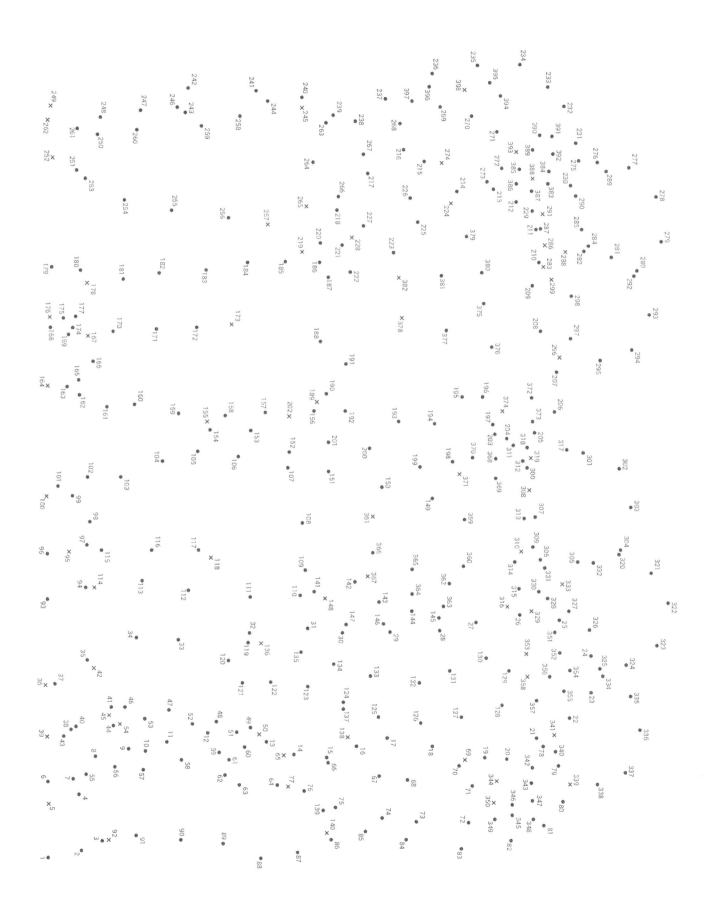

Figure 13

Figure 14

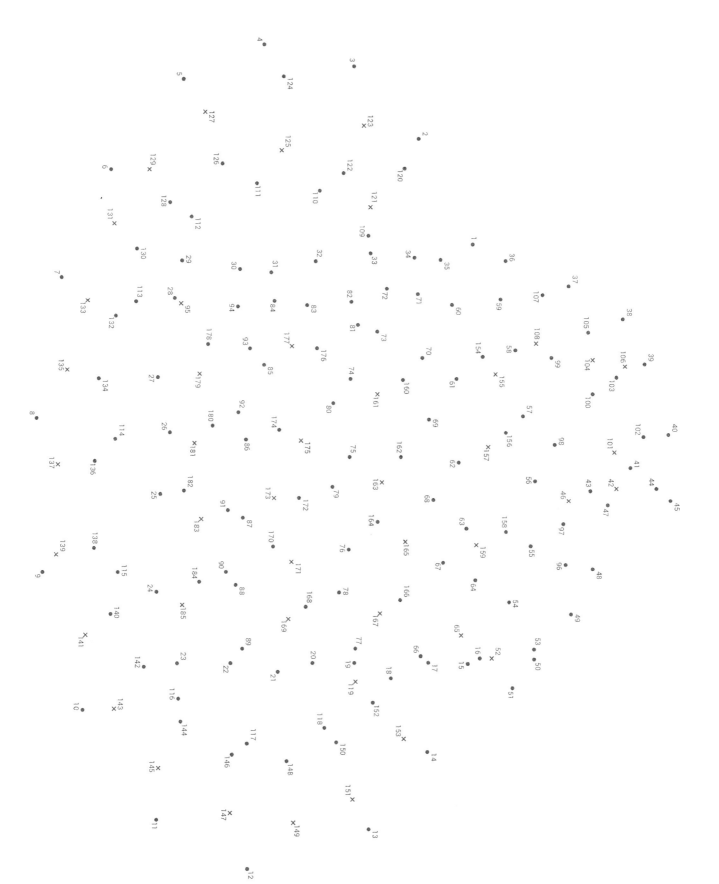

Figure 15

Figure 16

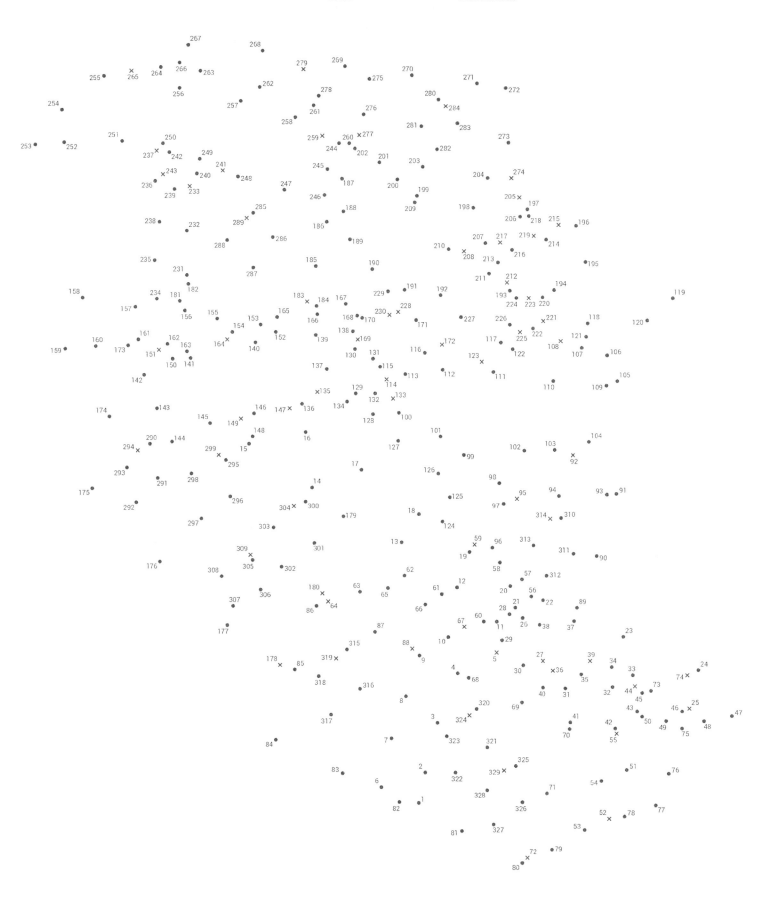

Figure 17

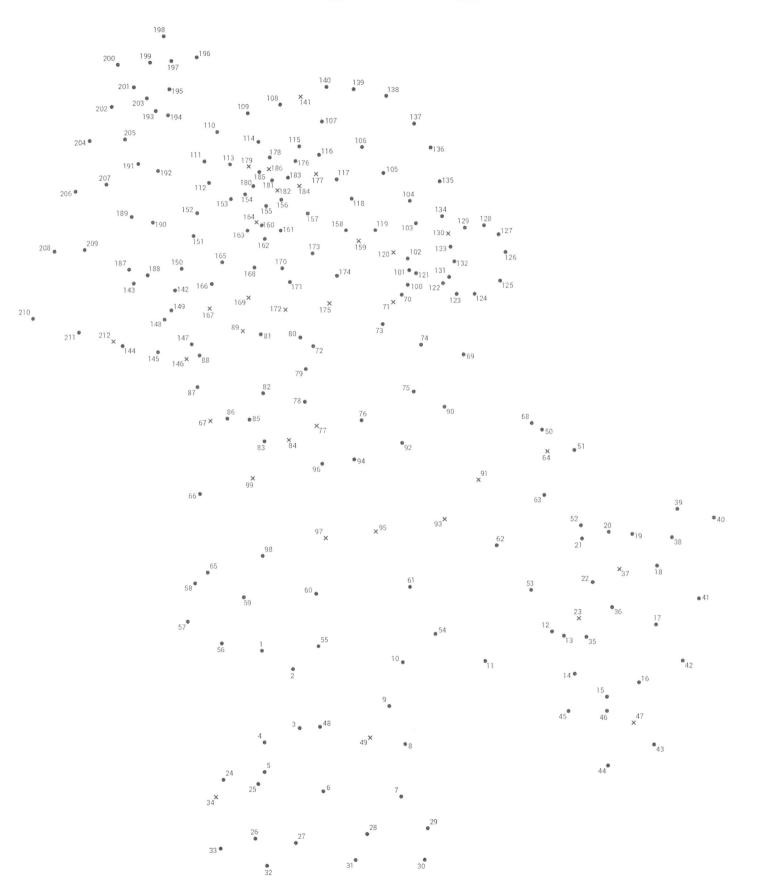

Figure 18

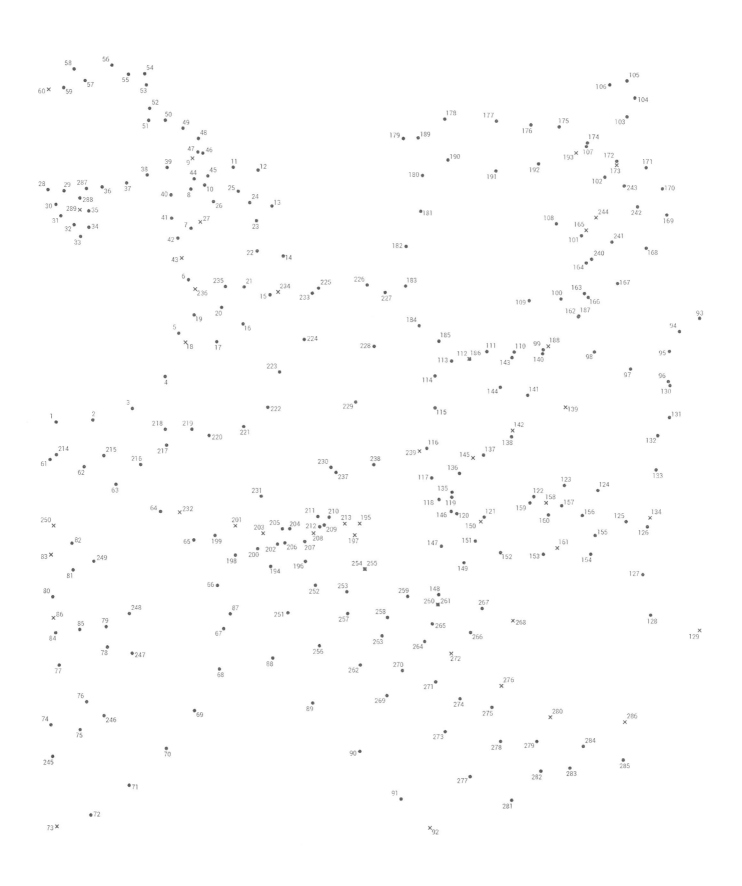

Figure 19

Figure 20

Super Challenging!

Figure 21

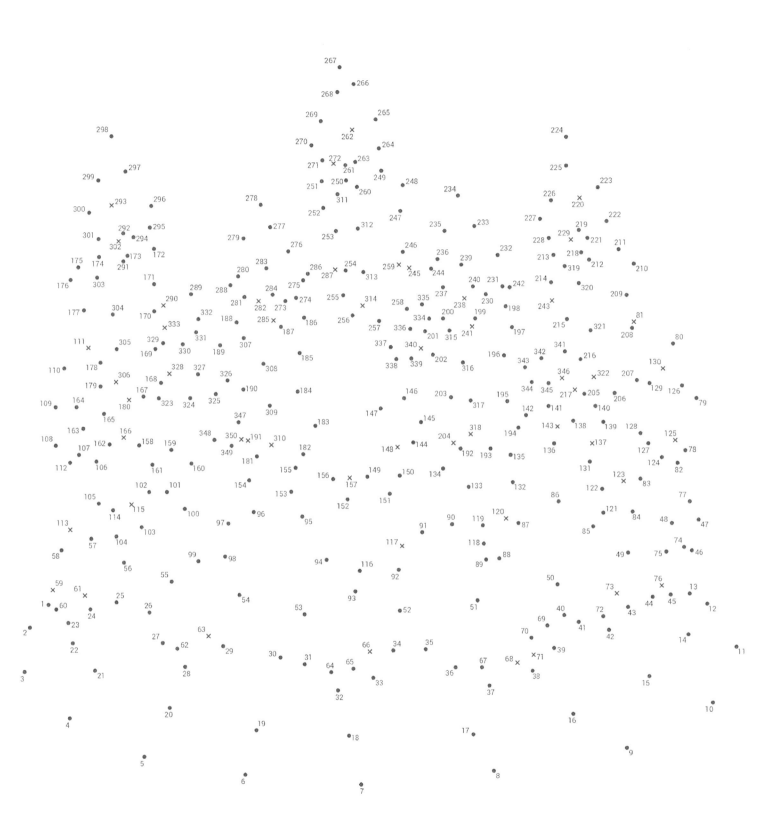

Figure 22

Figure 23

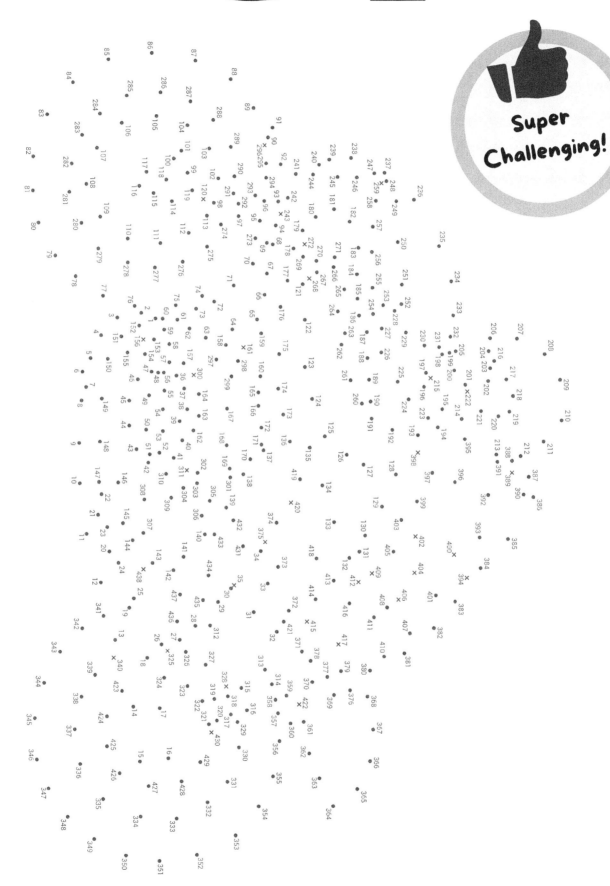

Super
Challenging!

Figure 24

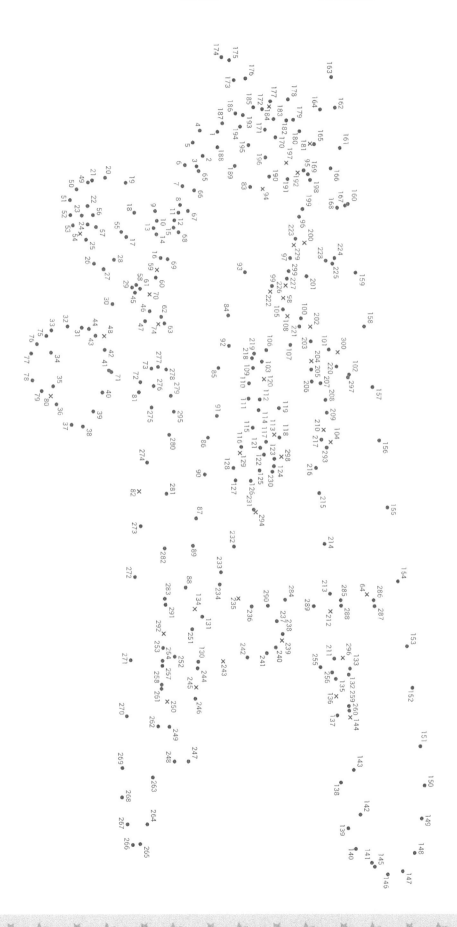

Figure 25

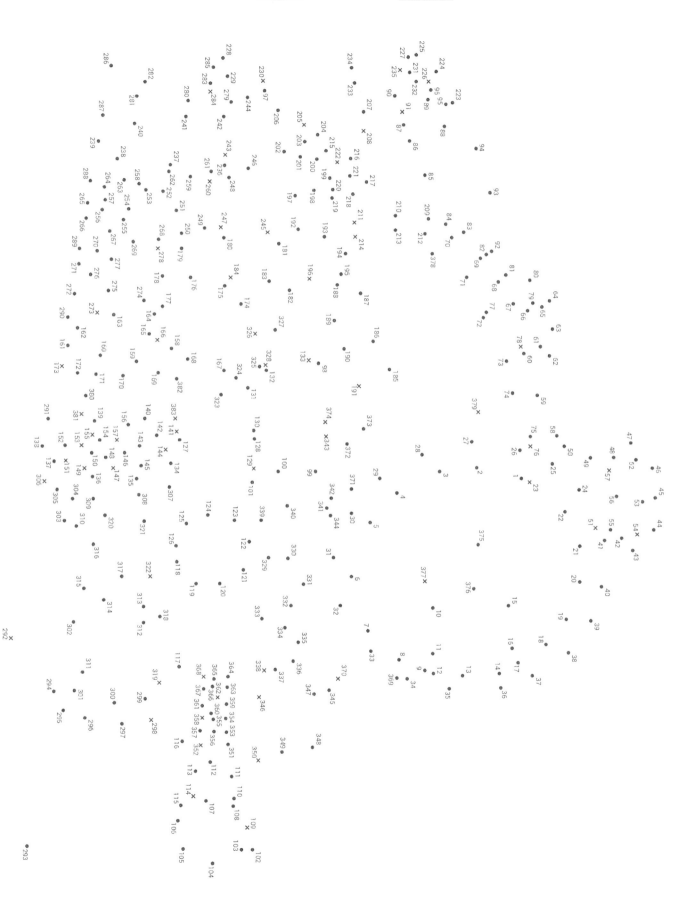

Figure 26

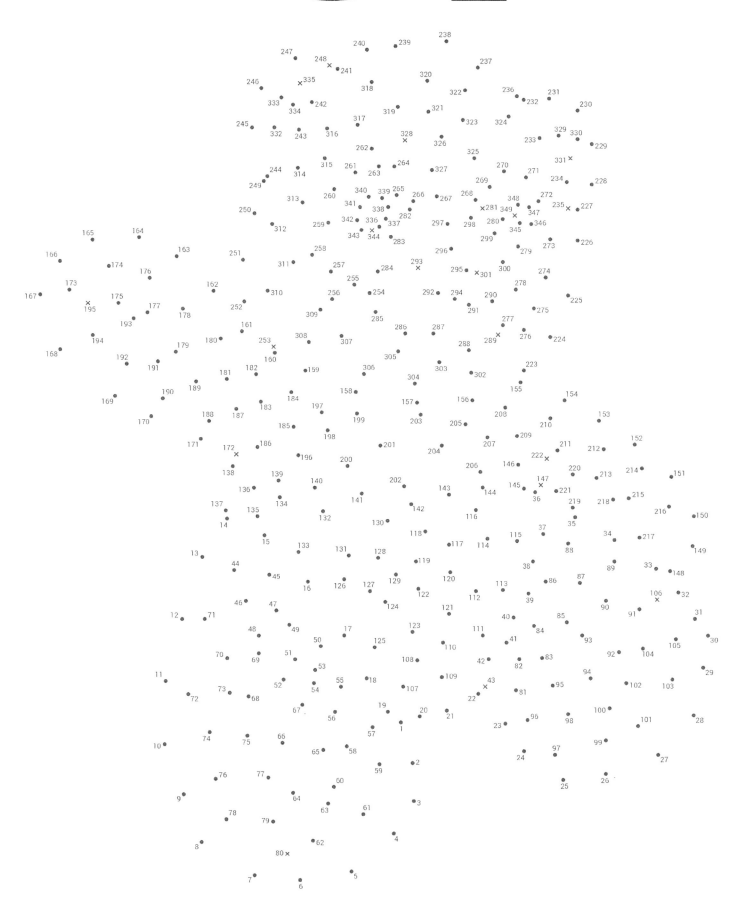

Figure 27

Figure 28

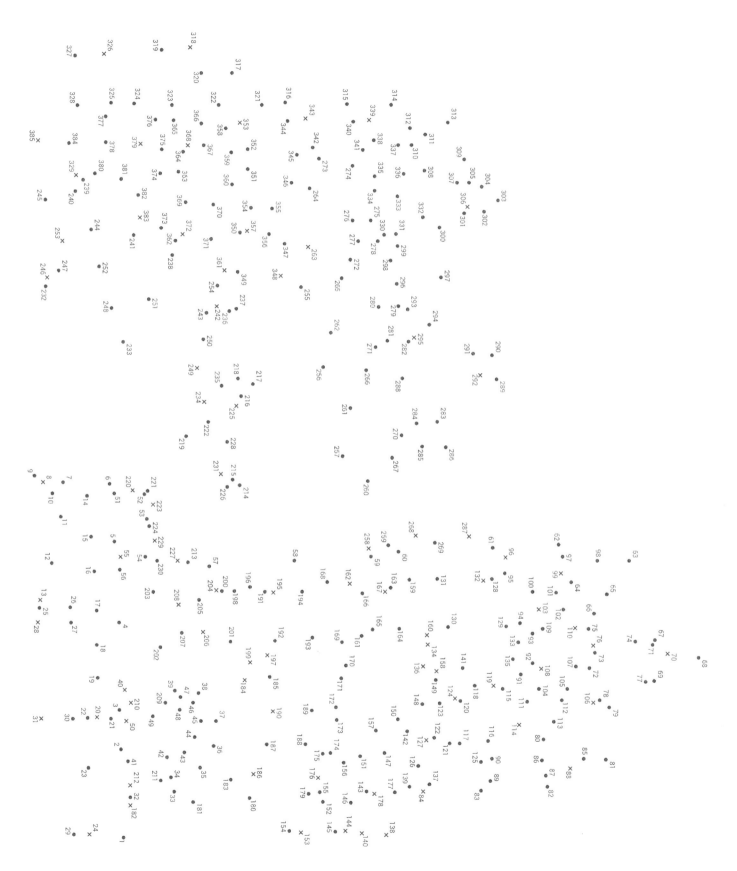

Figure 29

Super Challenging!

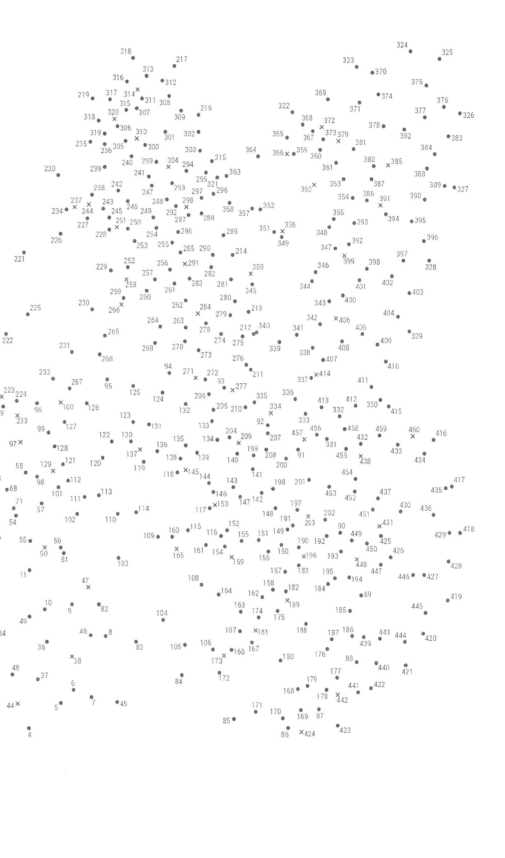

Figure 30

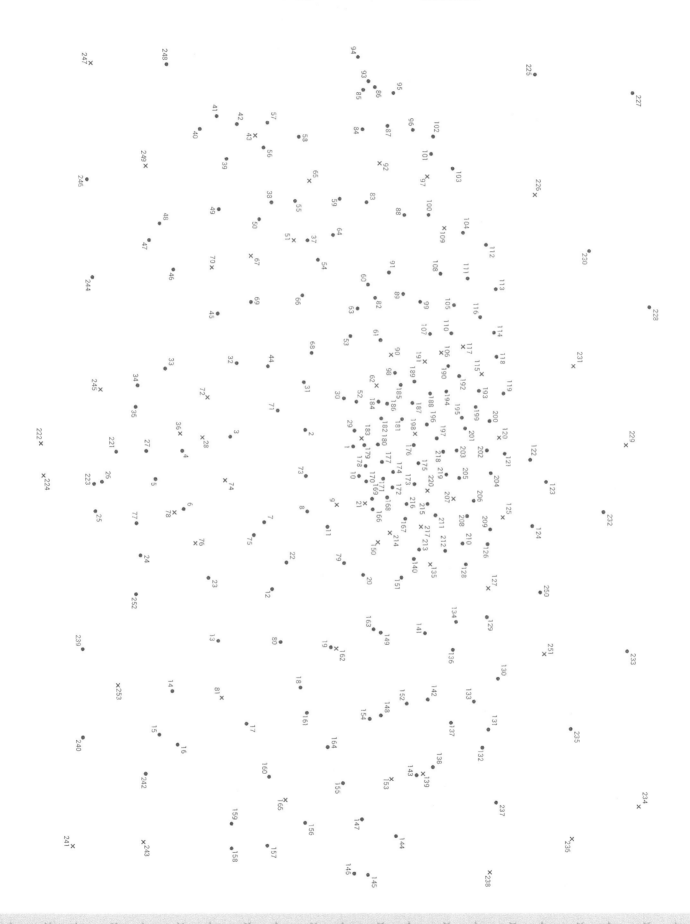

Figure 31

Figure 32

Super Challenging!

Figure 33

Super Challenging!

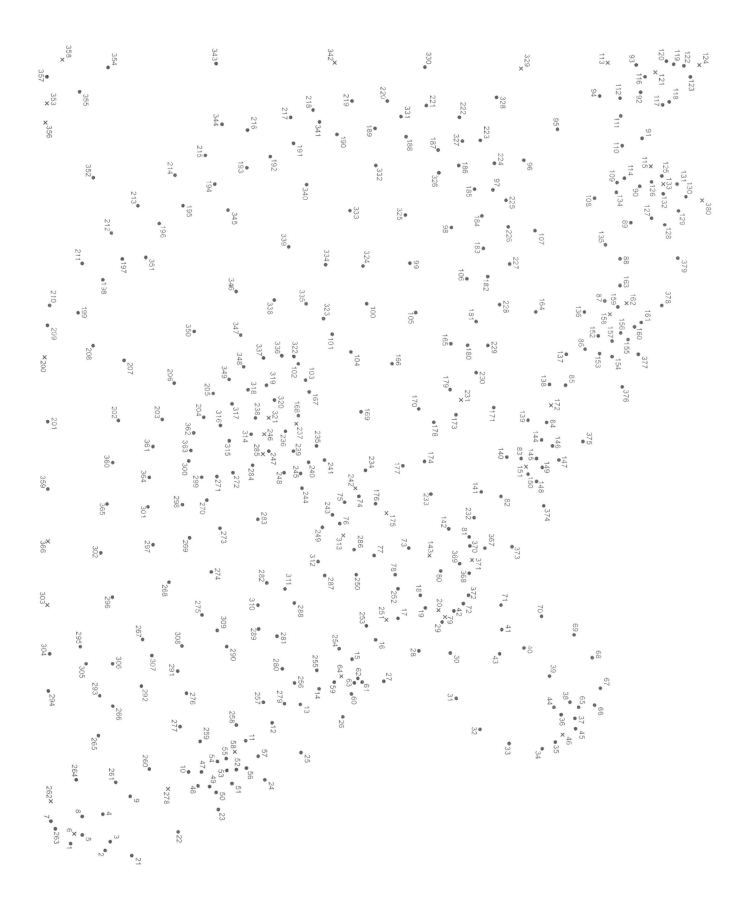

Figure 34

Figure 35

Figure 36

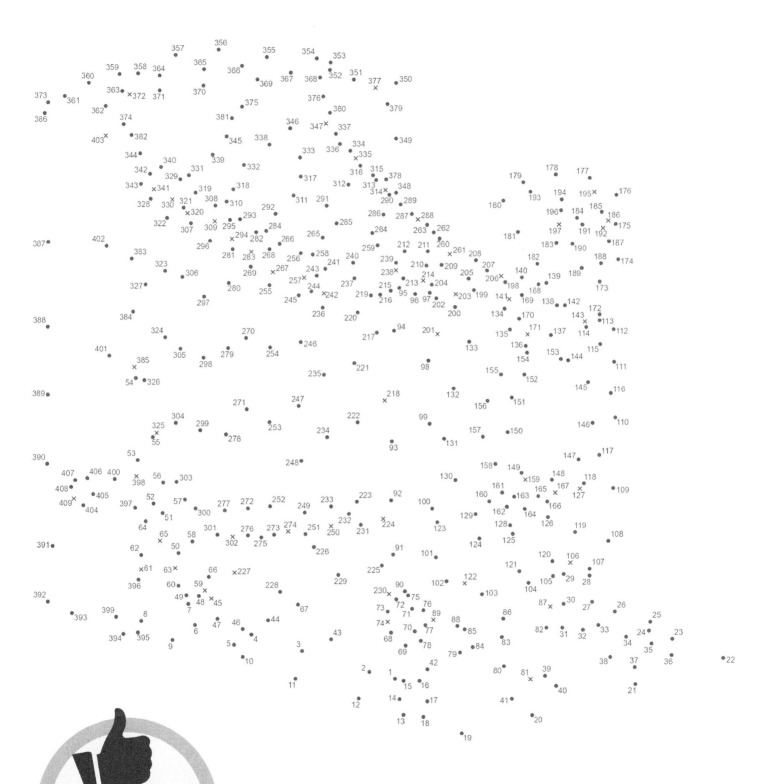

Figure 37

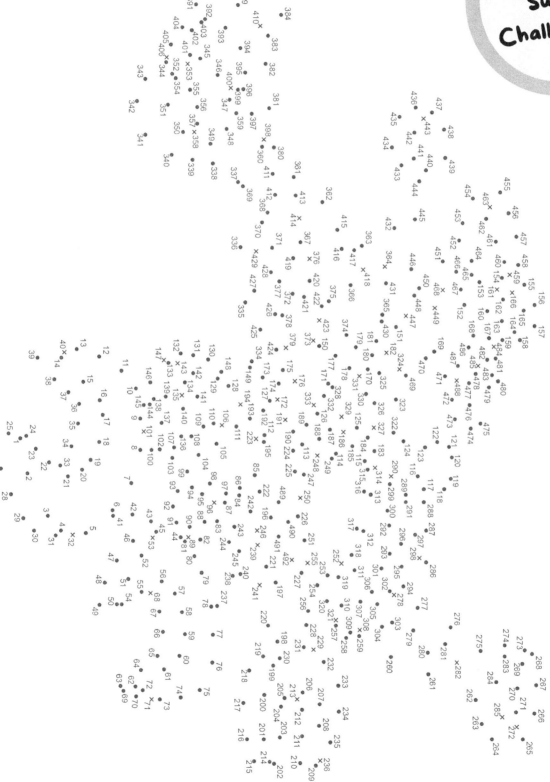

Super Challenging!

Figure 38

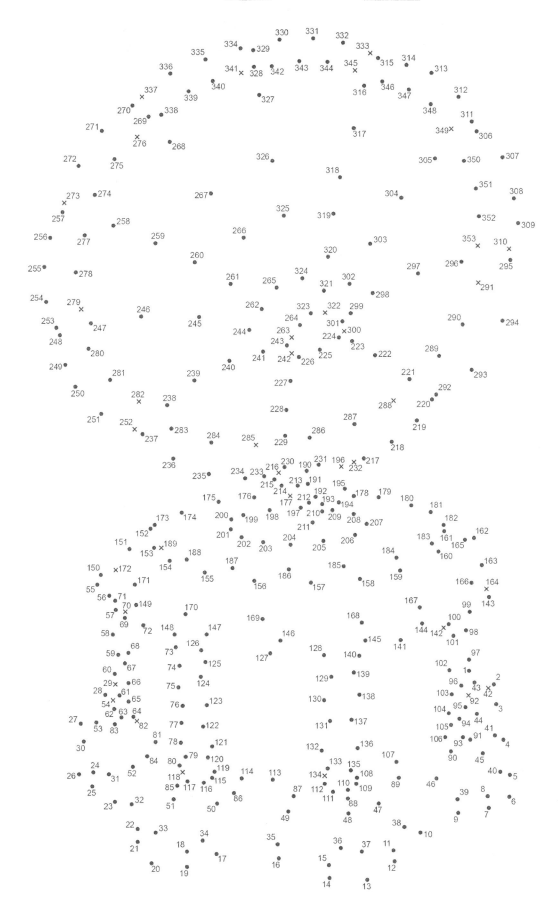

Figure 39

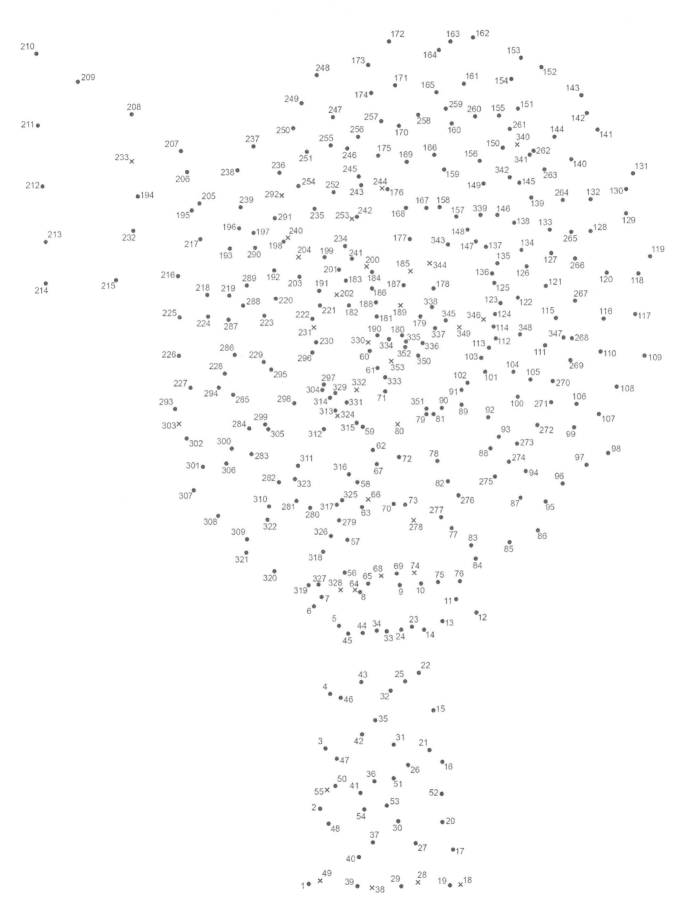

Figure 40

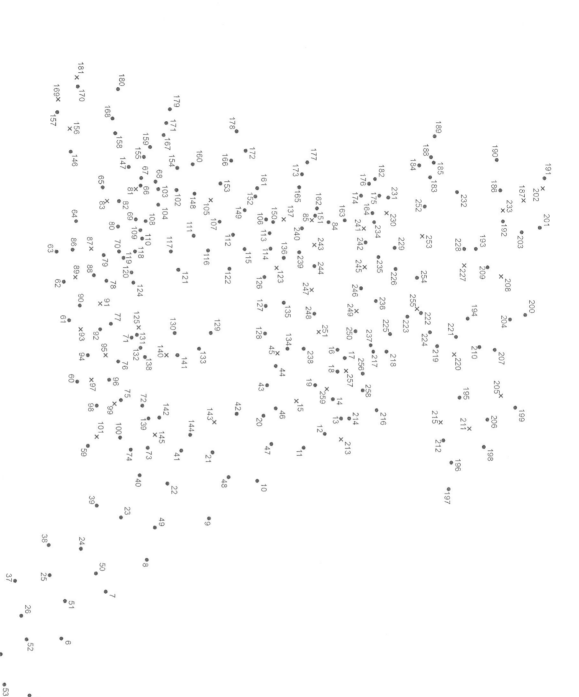

Figure 41

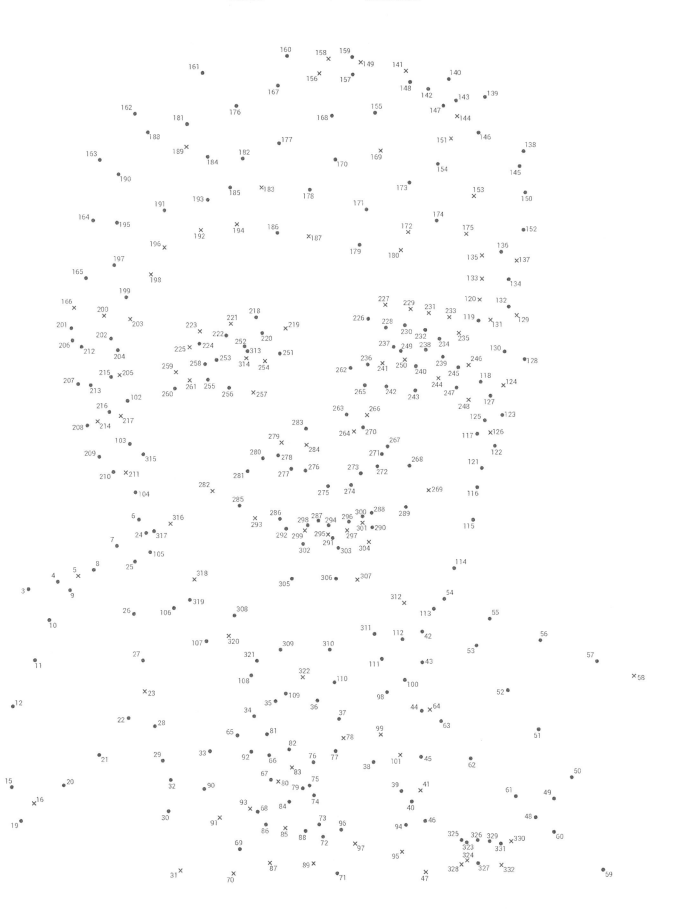

Figure 42

Super Challenging!

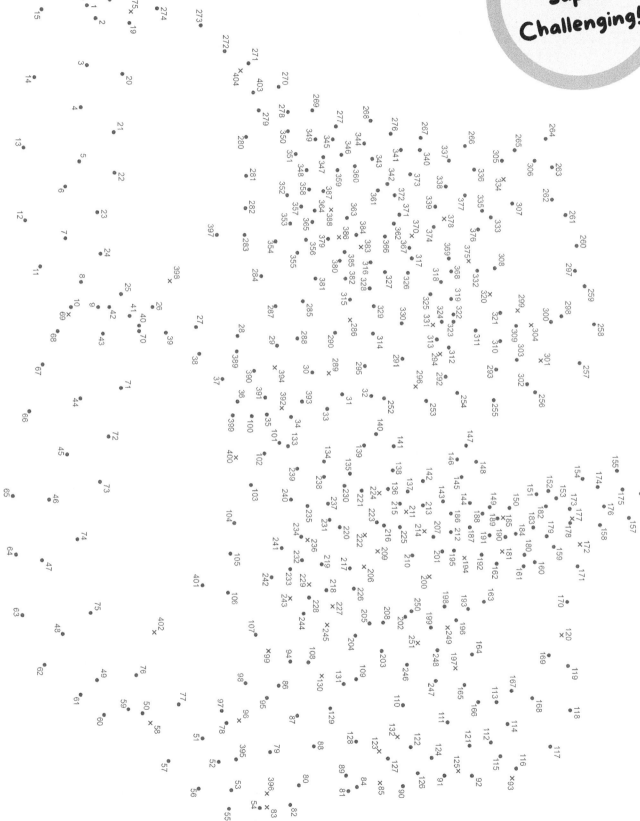

Figure 43

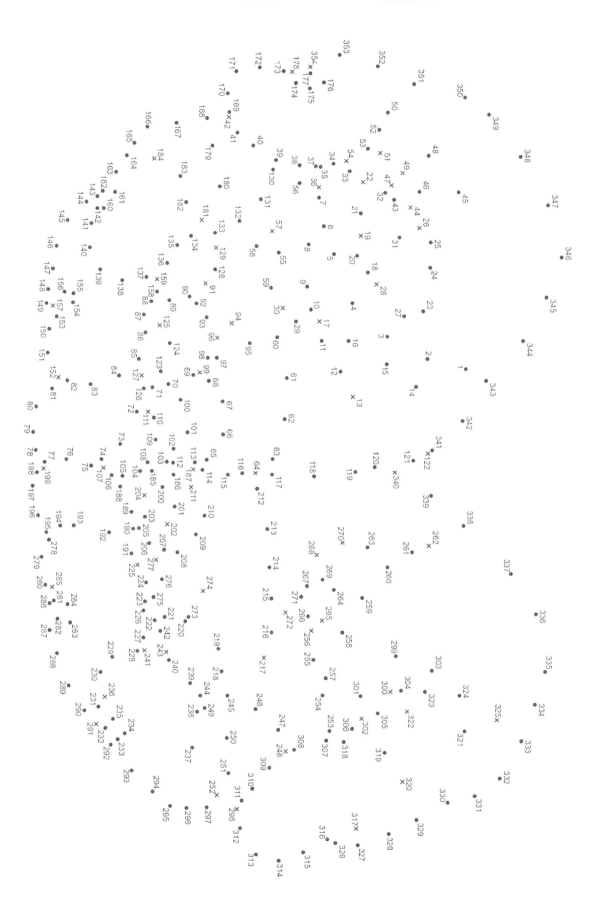

Figure 44

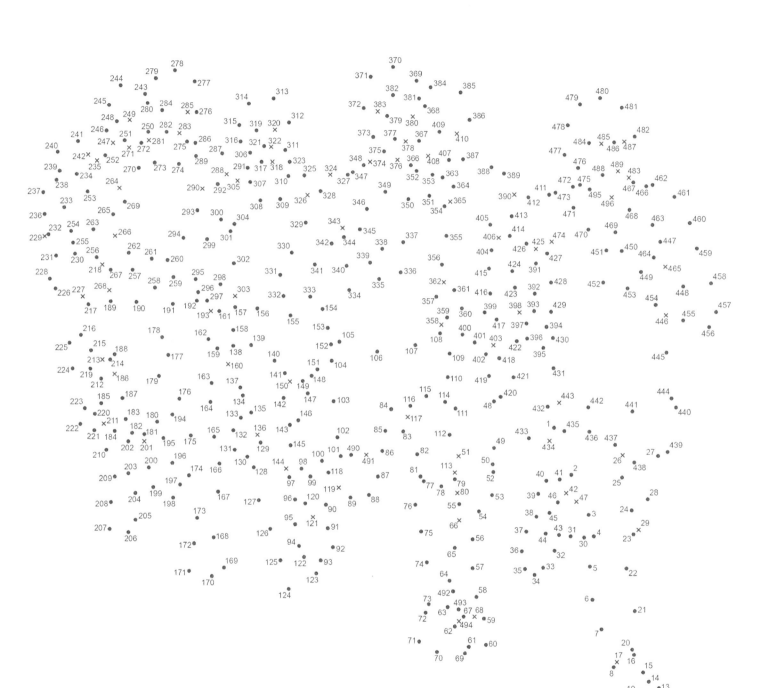

Super
Challenging!

Figure 45

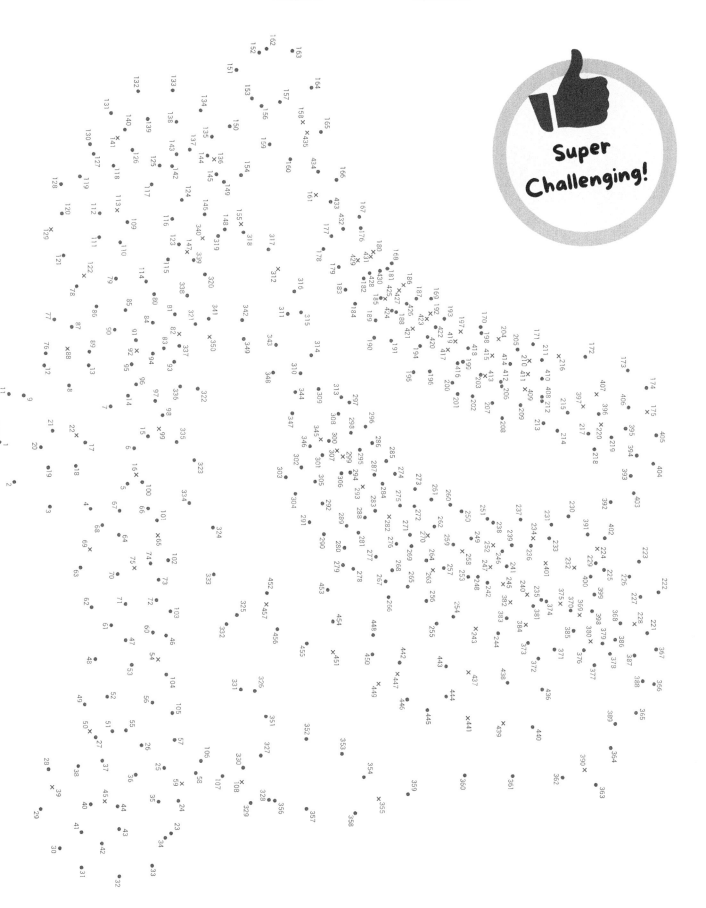

Super Challenging!

Figure 46

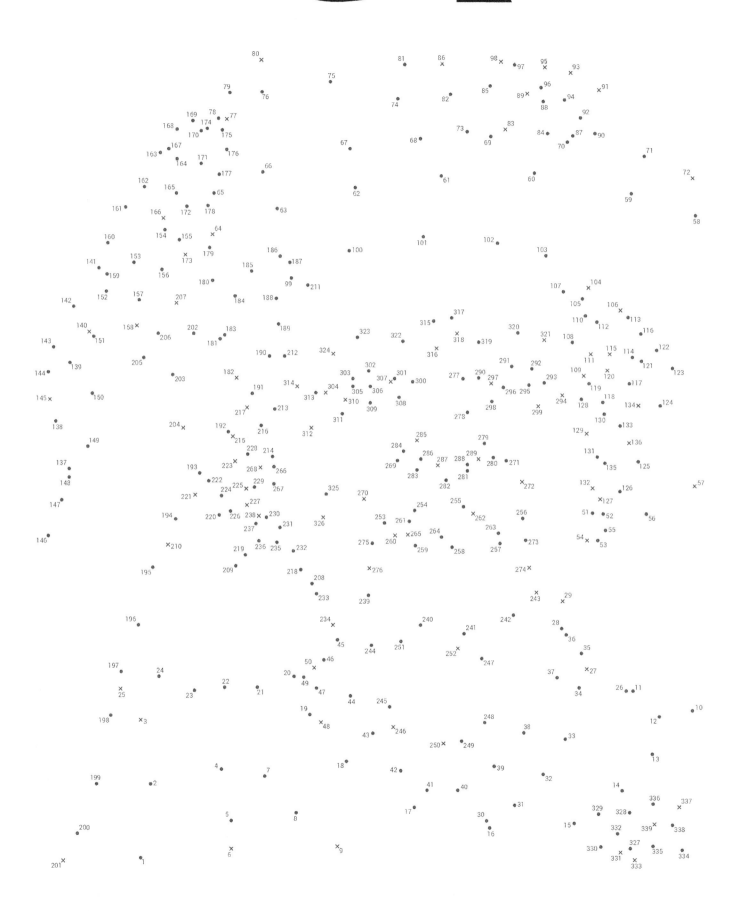

Figure 47

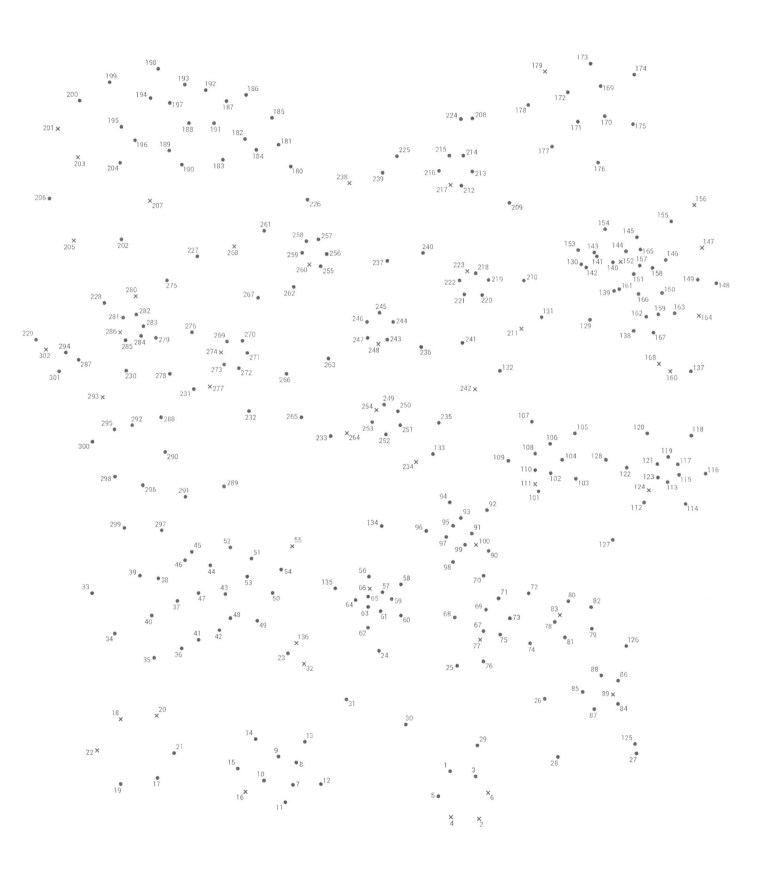

Figure 48

Figure 49

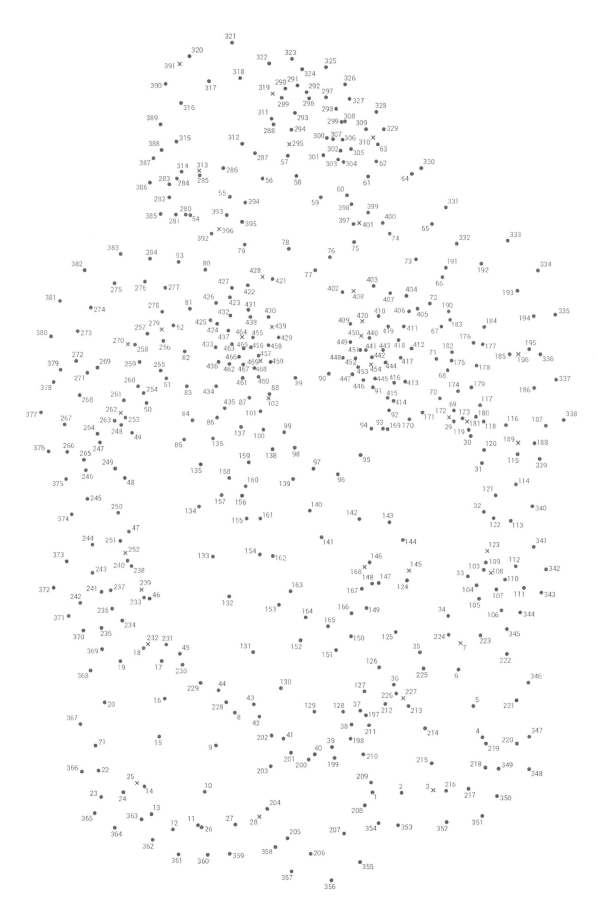

Figure 50

Super Challenging!

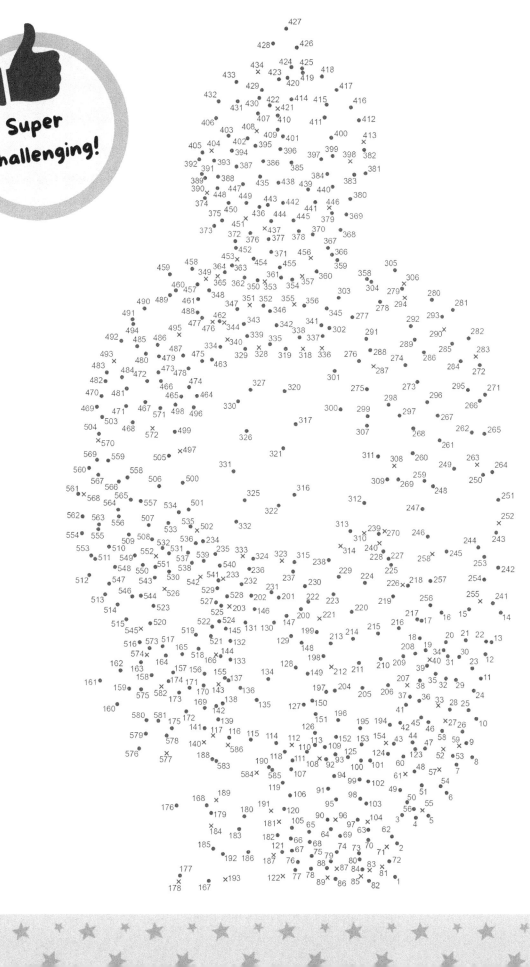